BE A CHURCH
DETECTIVE

BE A CHURCH DETECTIVE

A YOUNG PERSON'S GUIDE TO OLD CHURCHES

CLIVE FEWINS

CARTOONS BY TAFFY DAVIES

CANTERBURY
PRESS
Norwich

With grateful thanks to the late Revd Ivor Marsh and Jane Bingham FRSA,
without whose wide knowledge, advice and encouragement
this book would not have been possible.

© Clive Fewins 2005

Published in 2005 by the Canterbury Press Norwich
(a publishing imprint of Hymns Ancient & Modern Limited,
a registered charity)
9–17 St Albans Place, London N1 0NX

www.scm-canterburypress.co.uk

British Library Cataloguing in Publication data

A catalogue record for this book is available
from the British Library

ISBN 1-85311-628-9

First published in 1992 by the National Society and Church House Publishing.

Text design by *The Creative House*
Printed and bound by
Biddles Ltd

Contents

Church Detective Kit   4

Introduction   5

1. Why Churches?   7

2. Churches in the Landscape   10

3. Churchyards and Gravestones   14

4. Carvings and Corbels   20

5. Windows and Walls   24

6. Ceilings and Roofs   31

7. Tombs, Brasses, Paintings and Bells   34

8. Fonts, Roods, Cells ... and Mice   40

9. Lighter and Brighter – the New Plain Style   45

Glossary   51

The Church Detective's Notebook   54

CHURCH DETECTIVE KIT

Old clothes
Wellington boots

Notebook and pencil
Thin paper and cobblers' wax for copying inscriptions
on gravestones and brasses

Compass
Camera
Binoculars

Ordnance Survey maps (1:50,000 series)

A must for every serious church detective. Church crawlers should
learn to read an Ordnance Survey map in order to gather
fascinating clues about the landscape and places around their church.

Introduction

Just imagine it. Your local parish church has suddenly sprouted a large notice.

On it is written in large letters . . .

**COME AND SEE OUR UNIQUE
FOURTEENTH-CENTURY FONT.
FINE EXAMPLES OF MEDIEVAL SQUINTS,
CORBELS AND MISERICORDS ON VIEW.
ENTRY £1.50.**

The notice is so eye-catching that people start arriving in droves to see the church. Soon it becomes quite a tourist attraction and before long you and your friends decide to look around too.

Of course this is precisely what happens at many of our cathedrals and important town churches. But in the case of the 16,000 small parish churches in England, about half of which are medieval, I hope you'll never see that notice board.

Why? Well, for a start, wouldn't it be far more fun to discover all the interesting things for yourself before the crowds start arriving? After all, anyone can follow the crowd. It takes skill and imagination to be a special investigator.

Then there's all the fun and fascination of working things out for yourself rather than having them pointed out for you. Squints, misericords, corbels, clerestories, pyxes and roods . . . all these curious names will mean a great deal more to you once you've found out about them for yourself.

Fortunately churches have always been the sort of places where you can browse around for as long as you like, pursuing your own investigations. Sometimes there will be a guide book to help you. But often there is no booklet, or the church mice have eaten the last one, and you're left to do your own detective work.

So where do you begin? The aim of this book is to show you how to conduct your own investigations and to point out some of the fascinating discoveries that can be made. Above all, detective work should be fun. And once you've started on the trail you'll find yourself in some surprising places learning some really amazing things.

People who carry out their own detective work in old churches are often known as 'church crawlers'. This is a good name because you may have to get into all sorts of corners to discover bits of information about the building. Some of the most extraordinary medieval carvings are found very low down or very high up.

One of the best ways to work out the original plan of a church is to walk around its walls, beating back the brambles as you go! Once you've gathered all your clues you can start piecing them together to create a picture of the church's original builders and the people who worshipped there centuries ago. Take a close look at those tombs and carvings, windows and wall paintings, and you'll end up with a remarkably accurate idea of what made your ancestors tick. Tucked away in our parish churches are the clues to the lives, loves, wars and jokes of ordinary people five hundred or more years ago. All you need to know is where and how to look for the clues.

Once started on your career as a church detective, you'll end up with a wealth of knowledge that you could never have learned at school. You might even succeed in getting your parents hooked, if they're not church crawlers already. And they could prove very useful when you need transporting to other churches. After all, every Sherlock Holmes needs a Watson!

Armed with this book, your church detective kit and a little luck, you could be heading for the find of the century.

Chapter One

Why Churches?

One of the fascinating things about old churches is that there are always new discoveries waiting to be made. Beneath those layers of crumbling masonry and plaster may lurk remarkable secrets.

A few years ago a group of children in the Gloucestershire village of Sapperton were carrying out a study of their village church of St Kenelm. Their investigations led to the discovery of a previously unknown underground vault containing two coffins that had lain undisturbed since 1711. What a find!

And a chance shower of rain in Wenhaston, Suffolk, saved a priceless medieval painting from ending up on the rubbish dump. A few tell-tale traces of paint on some old bits of wood led a keen church detective to investigate further. The discarded planks were cleaned and then reassembled to form one of the finest surviving panel paintings in the country.

In the second half of the last century there was the amazing discovery of a tiny Saxon church in the Wiltshire town of Bradford-on-Avon. The original seventh-century building had been divided up into sections and put to all manner of uses, until the vicar found a clue which led to further investigations.

During the course of repairs to the building two angels were found carved into one of the walls. This chance find resulted, 14

years later, in the total restoration of the Saxon church. It stands now, much visited, as a monument to the enthusiasm of a remarkable church detective who acted on a hunch and came up with a truly spectacular discovery.

We need to go back even further than this however - to the sixth century in fact - to answer the question "Why churches?".

MISSION TO ENGLAND

In the year 597 Augustine was sent by Pope Gregory 1 to lead a mission to England. Augustine and his monks had discovered the wonderful freedom that comes from having a personal relationship with Jesus Christ. They shared this good news by preaching at special places marked with a cross of wood or stone. When more protection against bad weather was needed, and there was sufficient labour to hand, a church was built. The land around the preaching cross became the churchyard.

Some of the churches they built took on the shape of those first simple preaching crosses. After all, what could be more appropriate than the shape of the cross for the building in which Christ was to be remembered and worshipped?

Here the early English Christians listened to stories about Jesus told to them by the monks.

The more adventurous of them may have dreamed of going to the Holy Land to see for themselves the land of the Bible.

However, for most of them, travel was impossible. Ordinary people were rarely able to join the knights going off to the crusades; long journeys were very dangerous, and a trip to the Holy Land took many years to complete.

So if they could not visit the land of the Bible themselves, the next best thing was to bring the Holy Land to their own village or town. How did they do this? By building a church that became like a place of pilgrimage - a kind of pretend journey - to the Holy Land.

With these thoughts in mind let's take a walk around a typical cross-shaped church.

A CHURCH TOUR
We start at the *font*. This is quite simply a container for water. What it symbolises is the river Jordan, in which John the Baptist baptised Jesus before he began his ministry of teaching and healing. The font usually stands just inside the door of the church, as baptism is the first step in becoming a member of the Christian family.

Continuing our 'pilgrimage' we come to the *pulpit* where the minister preaches his sermon, and the *lectern* where the Bible is read. Both are key symbols in our pretend journey to the Holy Land. Through them we remember not just one place but many, for these are our means of following Jesus on his tours, teaching, healing and spreading the Word of God.

Christians worshipping in church are the disciples of Jesus and strive to serve him in the way he taught in the Bible. When Christians listen to the Bible being read and the sermon being preached they are symbolically following him in his early ministry.

Some churches have a *prayer desk* standing alone in the middle of the building. This reminds us of the 40 days and nights which Jesus spent alone in the wilderness. The person kneeling alone there praying on behalf of all the people in the church reminds us of Jesus in the desert, praying for the world, asking God for guidance and help to ward off the temptations of the devil.

Our route takes us next to the *chancel*. This is the area that would have signified to

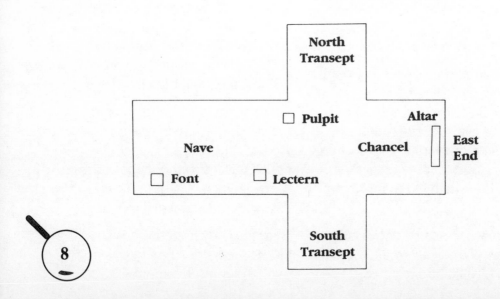

the stay-at-home pilgrims that they were approaching Jerusalem and the end of their pretend pilgrimage.

The *sanctuary* is the part of the church associated with heaven, and is therefore a very special place. Here we find the altar, the table at which Christians gather to receive the bread and wine, which in turn reminds us of the last supper which Jesus shared with his disciples before his death. The service of Holy Communion (or the Eucharist) is a special meal which unites Christians everywhere with one another and with their living Lord.

All church services are in a way like a pilgrimage, following various aspects of the life of Jesus. Perhaps the best example of this is Holy Week - the week beginning with Palm Sunday and the triumphant entry of Jesus into Jerusalem, through the dark days of Maundy Thursday and Good Friday to the waiting of Holy Saturday and the final triumph of Jesus' Resurrection on Easter Sunday.

Our pilgrimage has now taken us all round the church and on a journey through the Holy Land which Jesus knew. As we walk back towards the west of the church we will leave through the porch. In some of our great cathedrals and larger parish churches the porch is referred to as the *Galilee.* This is a reminder that Jesus worked most of his miracles and did most of his teaching in the region of Lake Galilee. As the Christian passes through the porch he is reminded that his own personal Galilee is the world outside. In reality his pilgrimage has just begun, for he must pursue it in his daily life, perhaps regularly casting his eye back to the soaring church spire which reminds him to fix his sights on heaven.

Chapter Two

Churches in the Landscape

As soon as you've sighted a church, your detective work can begin, even from several miles away.

Does it have a spire or a tower? What style is it? What materials is it made from? And why is the church positioned where it is?

Answer these questions and you'll have made some very important deductions.

FIRST, SPOT YOUR TOWER . . .

Towers and spires come in a variety of different styles and were built in different ways for very good reasons. Once you've identified your tower's age and type, ask yourself why it was built that way. Why are Saxon towers thick-walled and solid with small windows, and why should fifteenth-century town churches boast such excessively tall and slender spires?

FACT BOX: TOWERS

Saxon (c.600-1066) towers are small with narrow belfry openings divided by columns known as balusters.

Norman (c.1066-1200) towers are massive with small round-headed openings, usually surrounded by carving.

Early English (1200-1300) towers are much less massive than their Norman predecessors. They have supporting buttresses and slender, pointed windows.

Decorated (1300-1350) towers are generally tall and slender with buttresses placed at angles to the tower corners. Window openings are large and elaborate. Towers are often decorated with niches and pinnacles.

Perpendicular (1350-1660) towers are divided into several stages with large windows, and many tiered buttresses. They are often decorated with niches, carved panelling and pinnacles.

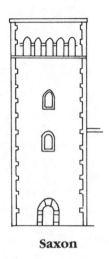

Saxon

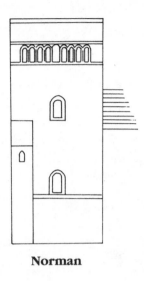

Norman

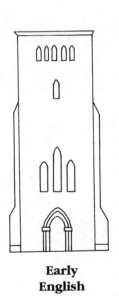

Early English

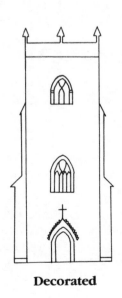

Decorated

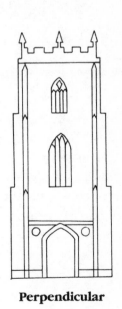

Perpendicular

11

THE ANSWER LIES IN THE STONE

Building materials vary all over the country. Look at the surrounding landscape and houses to help identify the local stone. How do the building materials affect the way the church looks now? Why are Cotswold churches covered in carvings? Why are north Norfolk churches so small and plain? Why do Cornish churches look as though they've been constructed from giant building blocks? The answer lies in the stone!

Building materials vary . . .

And what about wood or brick churches? This usually means that there's no good local stone available, but remember to look at the surrounding houses to confirm your deductions. Occasionally you'll find a church constructed from materials entirely foreign to the area ... and that should send you off on another detective trail!

FACT BOX: BUILDING MATERIALS

Limestone - Long lasting, often golden in colour, suitable for fine carving and building high. (Yorkshire, Derbyshire, Nottinghamshire, Leicestershire, Northamptonshire, Bedfordshire, Oxfordshire, Gloucestershire, Wiltshire and Somerset)

Granite - Very hard and difficult to carve, bluish-grey. (Cornwall)

Sandstone - Soft, orange-brown, suitable for elaborate carving but easily eroded. (Cheshire, Shropshire, Herefordshire, parts of Lancashire, Staffordshire, Warwickshire, Worcestershire)

Flint - Small stones of very hard texture, roughly squared and mixed with a type of cement to form walls. (Suffolk, Norfolk, Essex, parts of Berkshire, South Oxfordshire, Buckinghamshire, Hertfordshire, Wiltshire, Hampshire, Surrey, South Sussex, Kent)

Wood - Used in Saxon churches. (Found in areas lacking good building stone such as Essex and the Home Counties)

Brick - Used by Saxon and Tudor masons but primarily by the Victorians who exploited its decorative potential.

CHURCHES AND THEIR POSITIONS

Churches, like villages, were often built on hills for reasons of defence, visibility and good drainage. Some hilltop churches are sited on ancient burial mounds. The most famous hilltop church to be built on a sacred pagan site is St Michael's Church, at the top of Glastonbury Tor. Hilltop churches are often dedicated to St Michael, the archangel and dragon slayer.

Churches are also often found near rivers. One reason for this is accessibility, but water has a sacred significance too.

Many sacred pagan sites were associated with water and the early church builders often deliberately adopted these sites.

CHURCHES THAT STAND ALONE

Some country churches stand alone, perhaps in fields, far away from the nearest village. Perhaps there was once a village surrounding the building, but because of the plague, or a fire or some other reason it disappeared.

Perhaps the building was deliberately positioned away from the village - as a rival to an existing church, or as a result of a boundary dispute, or at the whim of a wealthy landowner.

Whatever the reason, churches that stand alone always present a challenge to the church detective who will want to know the reason why, since the vast majority of churches stand in central positions in towns and villages.

One little church that stands all alone in the middle of a field (and is still used) is at Wheatfield in Oxfordshire. The nearest village is a mile away, so why is the church all alone, approached only by a winding path round the boundaries of fields? To find the vital clues to the mystery the church detective first has to look at the name. "Wheatfield". So it surely must have been a farming community originally?

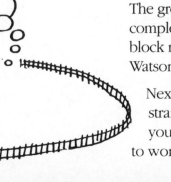

The humps and bumps in the unploughed fields that surround the little church suggest that there were once buildings around it - a whole village in fact.

Entering the church a keen pair of eyes will spot a series of monuments to the local great families - the Tippings and the Rudges - but these cease at the end of the eighteenth century. So at least we know that the manor house was inhabited 200 years ago. But emerging from the church the detective will notice something else - or rather the lack of it. There is no manor house to be seen.

There is no guide book in Wheatfield church, so the church detective has to go to other sources. In the case of Wheatfield the source turned out to be a book in the local library, but it could equally easily have been the local vicar, a churchwarden, or a parish official.

Wheatfield was indeed once a thriving village, with houses all round the church except on one side where there stood a large mansion. Around 1500 the owner of the mansion and of the other houses in the village enclosed the open fields and turned the land over from growing crops to keeping sheep. Then some 250 years later the squire decided to turn the acres surrounding his great house into parkland. He rehoused all the locals and razed the village to the ground with the exception of the little church which became his private chapel.

The great house was burned down completely in 1813 and only the stable block remains. Elementary, my dear Watson!

Next time you see a church in a strange position, try putting your own detective powers to work!

Churchyards and Gravestones

Detectives frequently start their investigations with a body. But the church detective in a medieval churchyard can be faced with thousands of bodies! Luckily all of them are out of sight. But they have left plenty of evidence behind them.

Why is the path leading through the churchyard to the main door of the church banked up so high on both sides? And why is it that there seem to be fewer burials on the north side of the church than on the other three sides?

THROUGH THE CHURCH GATE . . .

Usually the entrance to the churchyard is a simple gate or stile but often you'll pass through a small, roofed structure known as a *lychgate*. Stop for a moment and consider what this was used for. The chances are you'll be leaning against a waist-high block topped with a horizontal slab. A thoughtful detective will look at the length and height of the slab and deduce that this could be the place that the coffin bearers stopped to rest their heavy load.

Traditionally the priest met the coffin bearers at the church gate and the burial ceremony began here. Lychgates are associated with death and even to this day some superstitious bridal couples will enter the church another way.

As well as the lychgate there are lots of other interesting things to be found in churchyards.

Look around for a *preaching cross*, often centuries older than the church itself. If you're lucky you may find a *priest's house*, a *school*, a *lockup* (or one-man prison) and even a set of *stocks* - all within the churchyard walls! All these features are reminders that graveyards were once much more than mere burial places. Churchyards in the middle ages were the centre of parish life - market place, outdoor courtroom, education and leisure centre all rolled into one.

HELP!

THE BODIES

But what about the bodies? Why are they buried where they are? It's easiest to solve this problem when the sun is shining, but in the absence of sunshine, use your church detective's compass. You'll see that all the bodies point due east with their inscriptions facing outwards. You'll probably have noticed too that the church faces the same way, with its holiest point, the altar, at the east end.

But why east? The source of the rising sun had been worshipped by people of primitive religions for centuries whereas Christians look to the east as the site of the holy city of Jerusalem.

And why is the ground banked up so high in some sections of the churchyard? Could it be that at some stage in the past there has been a mass burial? Perhaps as a consequence of a local plague or other disease that swept through the community? You might need to delve into your church detective's kit to find references to books and people who can help you.

Is the church perhaps near the site of a battle? Some churches were used as places of defence or safety in the English Civil War that lasted from 1642-51. Others were used as prisons. In several - both inside and outside - bullet holes resulting from the Civil War can be seen. In at least one, a cannonball fired by the Roundhead forces that were attacking the town is still lodged in the outside wall of the building.

Why do there seem to be fewer burials on the north side of the building? Look where the church's shadow falls and you'll have the answer. In the middle ages, people feared that dark places were inhabited by the devil. Only the lowest members of society were laid to rest in the shadows. Strangers, criminals, suicides and highwaymen were the only ones buried on the north side of the church. Restrict your search to the dark side if you're on the look out for scoundrels!

GRAVESTONES GALORE

In medieval times the poor were simply buried in the ground, often without a coffin, one on top of another over the centuries. This is why the floor level in many old churches is sometimes lower than that of the surrounding churchyard outside.

Wealthy or important people were often commemorated by elaborate memorials, sometimes grouped together in special family enclosures or housed in extraordinary buildings known as mausoleums.

Churchyard *tombstones* came into widespread use from the early years of the seventeenth century. The earlier ones are usually short, with dumpy, thick upright slabs, carved on one side only; later headstones are larger in area and thinner. From around 1700 the lettering improved greatly and you can find carved, scrolled and indented tops adding to the variety of the upright stones.

Apart from these headstones you will also find flat stones over graves, called *ledgers*. These flat stones discouraged body-snatchers because of their weight.

More ornate churchyard memorials dating from the seventeenth and eighteenth centuries are the *table* or *altar tombs* and *chest tombs*, with their solid sides. These hollow stone tombs often have gaping holes in their sides, half covered with weeds and ivy. They can be quite frightening if you expect to see grinning skulls inside. In fact there never were bodies in chest tombs. The burials were always below ground, just like those graves with a headstone.

The finest examples of chest tombs are to be found in the Cotswolds. The wealthy wool towns of the region also developed a variant of the chest tomb known as a *bale tomb*. Instead of having a flat top these memorials made good use of the easily carved local stone to develop a fine curved top, like a baker's "tin" loaf.

Due to a lack of local stone, wooden memorials or *bed-heads* were popular during the 1600s in Surrey, the Weald of Kent and Sussex. You can still see iron gravestones in some parts of the country such as Coalbrookdale, Shropshire, and in the Weald. They usually date from the eighteenth and nineteenth centuries.

bed-heads were popular during the 1600s

STRANGE HAPPENINGS IN CHURCHYARDS

Local folklore often says that a ghost inhabits a particular churchyard. Such ghosts might range from ghostly black (or white) nuns to horses and chariots reputed to race alongside a churchyard wall, as at Stratton St Margaret in Wiltshire.

Legends such as these were often pre-Christian in origin and are frequently connected to superstitions surrounding All Hallows' Eve (31st October), when the spirits of the dead were said to leave their graves and return to this world for a brief reunion with the living. Country folk were so terrified at this time of year that they would bring food and drink to pacify the ghosts and burn candles to light their way across the churchyard.

Another reason why people are afraid of churchyards at night goes back to the gruesome trade of body snatching. This prospered in the second half of the eighteenth century but a law of 1831 eventually put an end to it. The trade arose out of the need for doctors to have fresh corpses to dissect for their research.

Body snatching was so rife in some areas that special watch huts had to be built in churchyards to house volunteers who would keep a round-the-clock vigil to ensure that robbers did not dig up newly buried coffins and remove the bodies inside. You can see two of these huts in the churchyard at Warblington in Hampshire.

In other churchyards "body snatchers' cages" were set up. These were iron devices erected round the grave and later moved on for use elsewhere when the corpses were too old to be dug up for use in medical research.

EPITAPHS

You can spend hours in a graveyard just reading the inscriptions on the tombstones. Keep a record of any humorous or particularly gruesome ones. Dig into your detective kit for cobblers' wax and plain paper and make some rubbings to take home.

Here lies my wife: here let her lie!
Now she's at rest, and so am I.

In bloom of life
She was snatch'd from hence
She had not room
To make defence:
For tiger fierce
Took life away
And here she lies in a bed of clay.

Gravestones are a wonderful source of information on how people used to live. A trip round a graveyard with a notebook can yield fascinating evidence on what jobs people did, how many children they had and how long most people could expect to live. You might come away feeling lucky you weren't alive a few hundred years ago, when so few children survived to be adults!

THE NATURE RESERVE

If you are a natural history enthusiast you might already know what wonderful nature reserves churchyards can be.

If there are old tombstones in your local churchyard look closely to see if there are any large areas of moss or lichen on them. There are all sorts of different lichens and more than half of the British species grow on stone. The ones you see growing on old tombstones, and on the church and churchyard walls, are likely to be the oldest plants in the neighbourhood.

Lichens are very sensitive to air pollution and grow much more freely in the countryside than in towns, so if you are a town dweller and your church is an old one the church building and tombstones are likely to provide your only chance of observing these long-lived plants.

If there is an area of your churchyard where the grass is hardly ever mown, imagine what might be living there? Foxes? Deer? Snakes, if the soil is light and sandy? Maybe you won't find deer or snakes if you live in a town, however big your churchyard, but all sorts of rare birds such as kestrels and goldcrests have been found nesting in town churchyards.

Church detectives who live in towns may well find many species of plant that are not seen elsewhere in the locality - merely because there is no keen gardener whose hoe prevents the seeds from getting established. Don't forget too that many seeds dropped by passing birds or carried by the wind will probably stand a better chance of survival in a churchyard than in a garden.

Also you'll find all manner of butterflies and a large number of small mammals. Of course, if the land has never been cultivated the church detective with an interest in rare plants will literally have a field day.

Contrary to popular belief, belfries are not good places in which to find bats. They are usually too dusty and full of cobwebs - and too noisy! It is church porches where you are far more likely to find bats. Sharp-eyed church detectives may spot bat droppings on the church floor. They resemble mouse droppings, but are drier, and more crumbly and odourless. Bat experts can tell different species of bat from their droppings.

many species of plant that are not seen elsewhere . . .

18

THROUGH THE CHURCH GATE AGAIN

Your investigations don't need to come to an end just because you've left the churchyard behind. Armed with a notebook and names of local families, you could carry your investigations into the high street and see if you can recognise any of the names above the shop fronts. Or consult a witness who has lived in the community for a long while. Maybe the Bakers are still selling bread, or the Smiths running the ironmongers's shop, just as they did years ago?

One day you might even come across some stones with your own surname carved on them (many people know where some of their ancestors are buried). And that could set you off on a fascinating family trail!

Chapter Four

Carvings and Corbels

Watch out for faces in unusual places. You may have thought that a church was just four walls. But these walls have eyes . . . and ears . . . and noses . . .

Hidden in the most surprising places can be a riotous cast of characters . . . two-headed monsters and man-eating giants, jesters and drunkards, wicked women and wild men of the woods . . . but you'll have to be a good detective to find them.

BOO!

Stand outside a medieval church and let your eyes travel upwards. Crouched under roof-supports, clinging to arches and doorways, and even guarding the drainpipes are groups of peculiar characters and animals known as grotesques and gargoyles.

But what are these suspicious looking characters doing lurking outside a house of God? Nobody has come up with the perfect answer. Some say that these mysterious creatures are survivals from pagan religions. Others believe that the carvings were intended to ward off evil spirits - certainly most of them are ugly enough! Whatever the reason, grotesque carvings have become a part of the structure of many churches and are still carved today.

FACT BOX: GARGOYLES

Look in particular at the tower if the church has one and on the upper parts of exterior walls.

Splendid examples can be found at:

Evercreech and Monksilver, Somerset
Patrington, North Humberside
East Markham, Nottinghamshire
Wye, Kent
Denford and Welford, Northamptonshire

THE GREEN MAN

We know quite a lot about one of these figures that appears regularly in old stone carvings in and on churches. It is the figure of a man's face peering through a mask of leaves which often spring from the corners of his mouth. This "green man" was a popular piece of folklore in medieval times. He represents fertility and the passing of the seasons and dates back to pre-Christian times when trees were often worshipped.

Carvings of foliage can also be found at some churches. At Adderbury, Oxfordshire, weird animals and birds are to be found in the leaves and flowers, together with figures playing musical instruments.

BINOCULARS AND WATERFALLS

Try taking a pair of binoculars with you to look in detail at the carving on the many stone *gargoyles*. These are the projecting water spouts that carry water from the roof gutters to the ground keeping it away from the church wall. If it has been raining you can usually see the water pouring out - from their mouths. If you have never walked behind a waterfall you will get the same experience creeping behind the water cascading from a gargoyle's mouth when it is raining heavily. Be sure to wear a mack and waterproof hat!

CORBELS

Usually lower down on the outside of the church are the corbels. They are carved blocks of stone fixed into the church wall that are designed to support other parts of the building such as arches or weighty pieces of masonry.

At the wonderful little church of St Mary and St David, Kilpeck, Hereford and Worcester, there is the most marvellous *corbel table*. It is a band of projected stonework that supports the roof timbers, and the stone corbels that support it are some of the most weird and wonderful to be found in the entire country. They are also some of the oldest, dating from the 1100s. The Kilpeck corbels include such oddities as a pig's head, fictional beasts, and any number of odd and slightly comic human heads.

Perhaps some of the faces were based on genuine living originals! What a way to be remembered for hundreds of years - by a sort of cartoon carved into a church wall. The same thing happens nowadays at Oxford and Cambridge colleges, where senior or retired members of the college are sometimes caricatured in grotesque carvings.

The next time you go up the tower of an old church or a cathedral look carefully when you reach the top to see if you can see any of the carvings close at hand.

When you are back at ground level look out for a carved sundial low down on the porch wall. With the help of a stick and a certain amount of sunshine you can reconstruct the times of the medieval services.

Sundial

Inside the church, carvings are usually (but not always) more restrained. Leaves and flowers, saints and angels are popular subjects, but don't be surprised to find a dormouse curled up at the top of a column or a man with toothache crouched on the ceiling. You can also find corbels inside the church - here they perform much and same role as they do outside, usually supporting stone arches that sprint off them to support, in turn, another part of the building. So you see, corbels are very important which is perhaps why so often they are adorned with grisly faces - to keep away anyone or anything wishing to attack or destroy them.

MISERICORDS
Try investigating the wooden seats where the choir sits. Are they hinged in the middle? If so, lift up one or two, you could be in for a remarkable surprise.

As any good detective will tell you, the clues are in the most unlikely places. What do the undersides of these hinged seats tell you?

Well, in the Middle Ages, when church services were much longer (and more frequent!) than they are today, the monks must have got very tired from standing for hours on end. So, the carpenters took pity on them and added carvings with ledges to the backs of the seats, perfectly placed for the monks to rest their weary rears!

These carvings were known as *misericords*, from the Latin word for pity. Not surprisingly, religion took very much of a backseat in these comic carvings! Under the seats you will find an amazing rogues' gallery. Jesters, jugglers, old crones, young lovers, wives beating husbands, foxes chasing ducks, monkeys masquerading as doctors, drunkards, knights on horseback and much much more, are hidden under the choir stalls in churches throughout England just waiting to be discovered . . .

MEDIEVAL GRAFFITI

You can find graffiti in the most unusual places, carved on doors and windows, inside window recesses, on sills and piers, and in other odd corners.

Some graffiti mark the registering of a vow, while some of the crosses cut in stone may have been made by pilgrims on their way to a shrine. Other graffiti might have been designed to scare off evil spirits.

In the parish church at Burford in the Cotswolds there is a graffiti scratched into the lead on the font saying "Anthony Sedley 1649. Prisoner." It was scratched by a young soldier, imprisoned in the church and awaiting his sentence of death for mutiny. He was eventually reprieved.

DESIGN YOUR OWN GROTESQUE OR GARGOYLE

Remember the difference? A grotesque is any carving, a gargoyle is a grotesquely carved water spout.

See if you can design it to incorporate a caricature of your brother or sister, best friend, or pet! Alternatively you could draw it entirely from your imagination.

Brother John was here MDCLXVI

Chapter Five

Windows and Walls

One of the first rules of building is that in order to go up, you must first go down. The best walls are those which have the firmest and deepest foundations, and one of the best places to view these is in the *crypt* of a church.

A true crypt is something very rare. So if you hear of a church with one, be sure to try and visit if you are in the area. Crypts are underground chambers beneath the church (usually under the east end) often originally built to house precious relics brought back from Rome or another centre of early Christianity.

One of the best places to view the early phases of a church's construction is York Minster. If you get the chance, do visit it. There it is possible to take an underground tour that encompasses the new steel and concrete foundations installed when it was discovered that part of the central section of the building was sinking under the colossal weight of the central tower.

Talking about a massive cathedral like York Minster is cheating a little, as this book is meant to be about churches and how to enjoy them, rather than cathedrals. But after all, cathedrals are only large churches - indeed some of them were large parish churches before being given cathedral status.

ANGLO-SAXON CHURCHES

The Anglo-Saxons, who built their churches between about AD 600 and 1100 left only small openings for windows and doors because they were afraid bigger ones might weaken the structure.

The earliest English churches were built from timber. When the builders moved on to using stone at first they were unable to cut and shape large blocks so they used rubblestone instead. One way of making small pieces of rubblestone into a reasonably strong wall is called *herring boning* (after the fish).

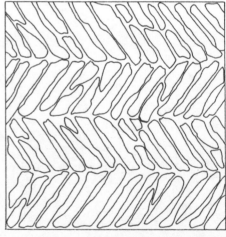

Anglo-Saxon herring boning

What the Anglo-Saxon builders did was to lay rows of stones diagonally, each row leaning alternatively to left and right, to produce a zigzag effect. This produced quite a strong result. To gain the extra strength needed at the corners of the building the Anglo-Saxons used large vertical stone slabs set alternatively with horizontal slabs.

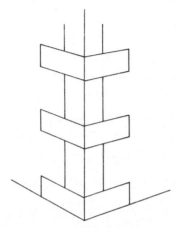

Anglo-Saxon long-and-short work

This is called *long-and-short work*. Both herring boning and long-and-short work are sure signs of an Anglo-Saxon building.

You will see good examples of Anglo-Saxon work at only a few churches in England, but fortunately they are dotted around in different parts of the country.

A very remarkable little Anglo-Saxon church is some 70 miles from York, at Escombe, in County Durham. You will need to be quite a good detective to find it, as nowadays the building is almost completely surrounded by modern housing. Escombe church is the earliest largely complete Anglo-Saxon church in England and is virtually untouched after 1300 years.

Another remarkable place for the church detective to visit is Wharram Percy in North Yorkshire. Here again you'll have to do a lot of detective work because Wharram Percy is a deserted medieval village still under investigation by archaeologists and the church is ruined.

However the way it has been excavated shows that the church grew in size and contracted according to the numbers of people living in the village. The archaeologists have been able to reveal the exact ground plans of former sections of the church, of which no part remains above ground.

What Wharram Percy demonstrates to the church detective is that if you know how to look for the clues - bumps in ground where they might have been a previous building, signs of a Saxon crypt, signs of a previously different shape, etc, - you will be a much more effective detective.

When you visit an old church, do pick up a guide book if there is one. If it is a good guide it might have a plan - or at least details - of how the archaeologists think the building grew - and probably contracted too - just like Wharram Percy church.

NORMAN CHURCHES

In 1066 the Normans arrived in Britain. They found the little Saxon churches rather small and gloomy but in their desire to improve and extend these churches the early Norman builders hit a problem. If you were to build an extension immediately outside your sitting room window, the back of the room would become very dark. The Normans realised that if they wanted to expand the width of a church, to let enough light in they also had to increase the height of the nave and put in new windows high up above the roof of the extension. This became the "clear storey", or, as the experts describe it, "clerestory".

Not all clerestories were constructed at this time. Many came later, in the first half of the fourteenth century. Church detectives can often tell when a clerestory was added at an early stage because the pitch of the roof is often less shallow and the exterior is covered with lead. If you look carefully you might be able to spot on the side of the tower the outline of a more steeply pitched earlier roof.

The Normans also had strong ideas on arches. These applied to both doorways and windows. Saxon doorways and windows had been narrow and bridged at the top with a flat stone. When wider openings were required the top was finished by leaning two stones inward on each other to make a triangular opening.

Although we do see some primitive arches in Saxon churches - especially in towers - it was the Normans who used them to greatest effect. They derived many of their building ideas from the Romans, whose architecture contained many arches - in theatres, baths, aqueducts and public and domestic buildings.

Some clever Roman architect discovered one day that if you made a semi-circular frame of wood between two stone uprights and then placed a series of stone blocks around it, their own weight would prevent the stones from collapsing when he took away the wooden frame.

Very clever! He had invented the arch . . .

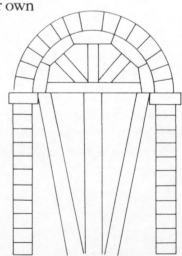

26

Today church detectives can recognise Norman work in churches by the magnificent arches - above doorways in particular. They are frequently characterised by row upon row of carved mouldings. Norman arches are not only seen in doorways but also in the wonderful heavy *arcades* found in churches of this period. Arcades are series of columns or pillars supporting arches.

By using these devices to support the building from the *outside*, the walls could be made thinner and more space could be used for windows.

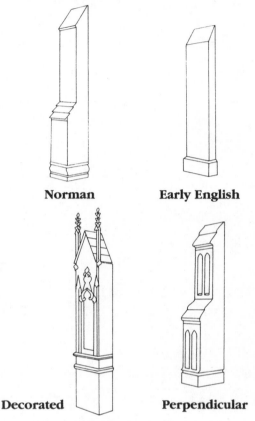

Norman   **Early English**

Decorated   **Perpendicular**

different styles of buttress

a Norman arch

THE EARLY ENGLISH PERIOD

Towards the end of the twelfth century a new style of arch began to appear. It arose when the architects (they were called "master masons" in those days) realised that arches could be pointed as well as semi-circular and still be just as strong. Using pointed arches they were able to build walls that were thinner and taller. Windows that followed the same pattern allowed in much more light.

The church detective can also recognise buildings of this Early English period (roughly 1200-1300) because *buttresses* began to appear on the outside of walls.

The decoration of windows was yet another way in which the medieval church builders could glorify God. By grouping together several of these windows (called *lancets*, after their spear or lance-like shape) in threes, fives or sevens to make virtually one window, often framed by a single pointed arch, they could create a beautiful new feature capable of carrying much more light into the church.

Early English lancet window

Another word for perpendicular is vertical and the churches for the next 250 years or so became characterised by their huge vertical pillars and even bigger flying buttresses.

A flying buttress

THE DECORATED PERIOD

It wasn't long before these simple window shapes changed to something far more exotic. Some in fact would say the sculptors and masons went raving mad! What they did was to use the gaps between the stone bars or mullions to form patterns, at first of simple geometric design, later of gracious curved and flowing form. Into these spaces of enormously varied shapes and sizes they inserted the most magnificent medieval glass. This great flowering of talent took place roughly between the years 1280-1350.

THE PERPENDICULAR PERIOD

In the Great Plague of 1348 many of the craftsmen working on churches and cathedrals died and afterwards there was a great shortage of skilled men. This may have been one of the reasons why a new style of building became popular at about that time.

The best comparison is with the modern steel-framed buildings built today. Great steel girders are bolted together and the framework they make forms the total strength of the building. When this structure is complete the floors, walls and ceilings follow. You can compare the churches of the Perpendicular period with this. With huge vertical *mullions* strengthened by horizontal stone *transoms*, the windows could be made enormous. The spaces between the windows are so slight that we wonder how the walls can possibly stand.

It was all a far cry from those dimly lit little early Saxon Churches.

The Church detective can also spot buildings of this period by yet another shape of arch. It was not a very practical design, but, with more and more windows and thinner walls there was less weight for the arches to carry. It looks as if someone has sat on the point of an Early English arch and squashed it. These arches were frequently set in a square-headed frame and so are quite easily identified.

The Perpendicular style continued right through the sixteenth century (see Chapter Nine) after the medieval (usually called "Gothic") style of building came to an end.

STAINED GLASS

Stained glass first appeared in churches in the twelfth and thirteenth centuries. The purpose was both to teach and to make the building more beautiful.

Early glass dating from these centuries is rare. The best of it is in the cathedrals of Canterbury and Lincoln and at York Minster, but very old glass is to be found in ancient parish churches in many parts of the country.

SLAM!

In these places you can feel something of the mystery that stained glass gives to an old church. It changes all the time according to the light conditions and often casts brilliant patterns of colour on the pillars and other surfaces inside the building. This can help to remind us of the light that God and his son Jesus Christ bring to the world. This message is reinforced in many of the stories told in the glass, such as the Beckett windows in Canterbury Cathedral or the lives of the saints we see in so many parish churches.

A stained glass window was made by fitting pieces of glass into a network of leads. The leadwork pattern was drawn out first on a large whitewashed table and the window was built up slowly, sliding the glass pieces in. It must have been very hard to get the colour balance right. You can see this for yourself by experimenting with a "network" of black paper and different colours of thin tissue paper. An alternative is to buy a kit with the network already made for you. A good craft shop will stock such a kit, which has little coloured plastic beads that can be melted and dropped into compartments, then baked in an oven to produce a stained glass effect.

HOW TO RECOGNISE MEDIEVAL GLASS

Often nineteenth and twentieth century windows look very like medieval ones. The designers and artists chose the same subjects and copied the medieval style (for example, saints standing on pedestals under canopies.) When you are walking round the outside of a church a sure sign that the glass is medieval is that it will have a silvery grey layer on the outside. If you follow these hints you will be able to spot the difference between the real thing and modern imitations:

Differences to look out for:

Look at the surface of the pieces. Medieval glass is bumpy and the bubbles go round in circles because it is hand blown.

Look at the reds (which should be a rich ruby colour). If you can see some chips of white under the red the glass is medieval. Medieval glaziers only had a very deep red and to make it brighter they put a layer of white glass under it. What they did in fact was to make a lump of white glass with the ruby glass around it. This is called "flashed" glass.

Look at the lines of the drawing, especially in buildings and backgrounds. Medieval drawing is uneven and varied. Modern imitations are far more regular.
If you can see the edge of a piece of glass you will be able to tell immediately if it is medieval or not. Medieval glass has uneven, nibbled edges instead of a clean cut. The medieval glaziers used clawed glazing irons to cut their glass.

How to tell early medieval glass (1100-1300) from late medieval glass (1300-1500)

Around 1300 a new technique was discovered for staining glass a pale, lemon yellow. This was called "silver staining" and it made a huge difference to the way windows looked.

By the use of silver stain, details such as hair and haloes could be painted straight onto plain glass. The result was much lighter, paler looking windows with larger pieces of glass.

Figures in early windows usually have pink or brown faces, with the hair as a separate piece. Later ones have white faces, usually with the hair painted onto the same piece.

Early medieval windows have small pieces of glass like mosaics, later ones have much larger pieces.

The main colours in early medieval windows are deep red, deep blue, deep green and golden yellow. There is very little plain glass and no pale yellow. From the fourteenth century onwards windows have lighter, paler colours, lots of plain glass and lots of pale yellow.

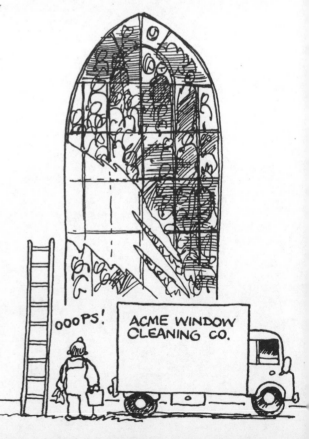

Chapter Six

Ceiling and Roofs

The most important word you'll need to remember here is *vault.* This is the word normally used for a ceiling built from stone and you don't need to be a seasoned church detective to realise that many old parish churches have the most wonderful carved stone ceilings. The actual roof of the church was invariably erected first and the vaulting inserted later.

The Normans achieved wonderful effects with their vaulting. Their arches are easy to identify - they are always rounded and usually beautifully finished. They also often have interesting zigzag patterns carved into them.

The arrival of the pointed arch in the *Early English* period meant that vaulting could be of varied heights. Columns in this period are thinner and often occur in clusters, forming a series of pointed arches known as arcades.

The medieval craftsmen put a huge amount of labour into building these beautiful ceilings. Just compare them with the insides of the roofs of most modern buildings which the architects are only too keen to cover up with fake ceilings because the materials the roof supports are made from are so ugly!

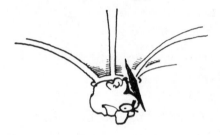

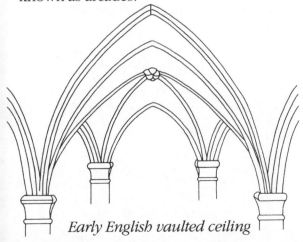

Early English vaulted ceiling

Many church ceilings of this period are adorned with intersecting *ribs* forming a rich pattern. Where these ribs joined, the builders often placed an ornamental roof boss.

In the 1300s as styles progressed we see the introduction of ribs that are chiefly decorative, rather than being an essential part of the roof structure. They were sometimes created to form elaborate star-like patterns, in which case they are known as *lierne vaults*.

A century or so later a most beautiful form of vault was introduced that can only be found in this country. This is the *fan vault*. In a fan vault all the ribs are of identical curve and are placed at equal angles to one another. The spaces between the cones or fans make diamond-shaped panels. Many of these fan vaults have the most amazingly carved bosses, but very often they are so high that the details can hardly be seen from the ground.

fan vaulting

WOODEN ROOFS

The passage of time has meant that the oak beams of many roofs in old churches have turned into a marvellous silver-grey colour. Many church detectives will wonder how the huge timbers were ever lifted into place all those years before modern cranes were invented.

The undersides of wooden roofs in many medieval churches are richly decorated with wonderful carvings and bosses. This is especially apparent in many of the churches of East Anglia and the West Country.

The main horizontal piece of timber that stretches across between the two side walls is called a *tie-beam*. They are often richly carved and decorated.

Where the triangular space between the beam and the sloping sides of the roof was quite small, the carpenters might fill it in with delicate open wooden *tracery*. This is a word that the church detective will meet again and again. It simply means intersecting ribs, carved in either wood or stone in windows or woodwork.

In many of the churches of East Anglia the huge tie-beams were replaced by *hammerbeam roofs*, mainly in the 1400s. This design required fewer intermediate posts to support the ceiling and allowed a wider span to be roofed.

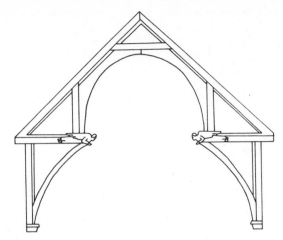

Hammerbeam roof

In East Anglia the famous *angel roofs* are nearly always hammer beamed ones. The beams frequently end in carved angels, with oak wings spread wide. There must have been a whole army of workmen who specialised in these lovely angels and who moved round the country carving them. When the worshippers looked up they must have felt inspired by this reminder of the angels that stood guard over them.

The other area of England where the insides of church roofs are outstanding is the West Country. Here *wagon roofs* are commonly found. Really these ought to be called ceilings because they form a complete "inner skin" under the roof timbers. They gained their name because they resemble the canvas cover of a wagon.

They are frequently divided into plain, flat panels or into sunken ones, carved with bosses and mouldings, and painted and gilded.

The roofs of many medieval churches were painted, as were the walls, and the church detective should always be on the alert for remaining traces of these paintings. If you come across a church roof that is very richly painted - particularly a wagon roof - don't be too easily misled. It may have been completely repainted in Victorian times. If the paint is reasonably bright and fresh this is very likely to have been the case.

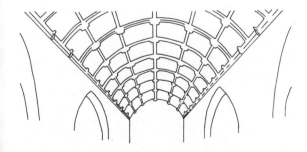

Wagon roof

Chapter Seven

Tombs, Brasses, Paintings and Bells

How often have you been to an old church and seen lifesize stone effigies of knights, lords and ladies, laid out, silent, as if they were asleep?

If you are a keen church detective, the answer will be quite often.

Some children find these effigies spooky - probably because they believe that the remains of the dead person are actually inside the effigy. Of course this is a mistake, but tombs inside churches usually do stand on the spot where a person of note was laid to rest.

At first only the clergy were buried actually inside churches, but later wealthy parishioners were sometimes allowed to be buried inside too. Memorials to these people are usually either in the form of large plaques on the walls, or tombs.

TOMBS

During the twelfth century tombs were simple coffin-shaped slabs of stone laid flush with the floor of the church. They often had crosses cut in them, and also symbols which gave a clue to the occupation of the dead person - for example, a sword for a knight, a chalice for a priest, or a pair of shears for a wool merchant.

The first life-sized effigies, recumbent upon their box-like *table tombs* date from the thirteenth century. Their poses are very rigid, and no attempt was made to give a realistic representation of the dead person.

As time progressed however table tombs (they are sometimes called *altar tombs*) became more elaborate, often painted or gilded, with effigies on top of them. A knight was always shown in full armour, his head resting on his tilting helm and his feet on his heraldic beast or some other animal. Most early effigies of knights are made from a dark limestone called purbeck marble, but alabaster (a kind of soft marble) was also used.

A few *wooden effigies* of knights and their ladies still survive, though as wood decays much faster than stone or alabaster they are very rare.

FACT BOX: WOODEN EFFIGIES

You can find good examples of wooden effigies at

Clifton Reynes, Buckinghamshire
Sparsholt, Oxfordshire
Fersfield, Norfolk
Paulerspury, Northamptonshire
Gloucester Cathedral

All date from around 1430

By the fourteenth century these tombs often had canopies and were set in a recess in the wall, though many were left free-standing.

Gradually the style of these effigies changed and they became less stiff and formal. By the fifteenth century they had acquired more lifelike poses and by the sixteenth century the figures on tombs are often shown leaning on one arm or kneeling.

In the 1600s and 1700s *weepers* became fashionable. These are small carved figures praying for the soul of the deceased, carved into the sides of the table tombs. They might be the members of the dead person's family, angels or saints.

The easiest way to date a monument is to look at the clothing worn by the figures. The changes in styles of dress worn by rich people over the centuries can be very interesting.

One church that is remarkable for its effigies is Aldworth, near Streatley in Berkshire. Here rest the "Aldworth Giants", nine much-larger-than-life stone effigies of the last representatives of the de la Beche family, who lived in a castle nearby.

BRASSES

You can see commemorative metal brasses on the floor or walls of many old churches. Like stone or wooden effigies they were a way of remembering a person from a town or village, and are particularly characteristic of England which has many more church brasses than the whole of the rest of Europe.

Taking rubbings of brasses in churches or at one of the many brass rubbing centres that have sprung up all over the country is great fun and is very popular among people of all ages. It is quite an easy task, using heel ball (cobbler's wax) and special paper - but it is difficult to do it well. Some people use old wall-paper lining rolls, but it is best to get the proper paper for the job. You can often buy this at a brass rubbing centre, or alternatively through the Monumental Brasses Society.

Brasses are most common in Kent, Essex, East Anglia and Oxfordshire, where many beautiful examples remain. In the Middle Ages the metal for the brasses was manufactured only in Flanders (Northern France) and Germany. The engraving, however, is English, and the English artists liked to cut out their figures and bed them in a slab of Purbeck marble or some other stone.

The oldest known church brass dates from 1277, and the finest collection is at Cobham, Kent. Like memorials in stone and alabaster, brasses can frequently be dated by the dress of their subjects. If there is an inscription it is also possible to date the brass by the lettering and language.

The keen detective will seek out brasses in the most unlikely places. They are often under mats and pieces of carpet for protection, so always pick up anything you can in an old church (within reason!). You never know what might be underneath!

STONE COFFINS

In some churches you may find some interesting examples of early *stone coffins*. These are often not as old you might think and may date from only the twelfth or thirteenth centuries. Because they are made of stone they are likely to have been the coffins of very well-to-do people. The poor had to make do with a simple sheet and no coffin at all. At the fine Norman church of Guiting Power, near Cheltenham in Gloucestershire, there is a great rarity - a tiny stone coffin that housed a child. Some people think it dates from Saxon times.

HEART BURIALS

When a soldier died in the crusades it was often very difficult to bring his body back home, so usually he was buried in foreign soil. Sometimes however soldiers asked in their wills that their hearts should be removed and returned to their village churches for burial. It is very rare to find an actual heart burial site, though at the little

You never know what might be underneath . . .

36

church of St Mary the Virgin, Hampton Poyle, near Oxford there is a hollowed-out stone in an arched recess that has decoration on the outside and a rectangular basin-shape cut out of it. This is thought to have housed a heart burial.

Far more common are the memorials to heart burials found in a number of churches. They often take the form of brasses and are usually shaped like a medallion containing the head and shoulders of a figure with two hands grasping an extra large heart. Sometimes near where a heart lay buried you will find a very small stone figure of a knight holding a heart in his hands. An excellent example of this can be found at the Church of St Mary, Bottesford, in Leicestershire, where there is a very fine collection of monuments.

WALL PAINTINGS

You may not have seen many wall paintings in the churches you have visited, but in medieval times they were very common.

Only a few members of the congregation would have been able to read or write so paintings were used as a way to teach the people about the Bible.

Some surviving paintings show scenes from the life of Jesus or scenes from the Old Testament, such as the story of Adam and Eve, whilst others are of well-known saints, like St George slaying the dragon. Others are more like diagrams. They were probably used by the priest to help the congregation get the point of his sermons - rather like a board used by a teacher. One of the most common of these "diagrams" is that of the Seven Deadly Sins.

You might even find yourself in one of the sixty or so churches where there is a *doom*, a painting of the Last Judgement presided over by saints and angels and the figure of Christ. Doom paintings can be very frightening - as they were designed to be - since they depict all sorts of evil people descending into hell. Artists really went to town in these paintings which were designed to make the congregation ask themselves, "Which side am I going to be on?". Most of the great doom paintings date from the fifteenth century.

Many of the common themes found in wall paintings occur in a number of churches, and experts believe that the artists who created the paintings travelled quite widely, practising their art. The finest paintings are to be found in the cathedrals of Canterbury,

Norwich, St Albans and Westminster but there are fragments to be seen in some 2000 churches up and down the country.

The exciting thing is that experts are gradually uncovering many of these fragments, most of which were painted over during the sixteenth and seventeenth centuries when they were thought to be idolatrous and primitive.

The people who painted over them did not realise that quite often the whitewash acted as a perfect preservative, under which the painting remained concealed, but quite safe - just waiting for the church detectives of a later century!

Beware of one thing however. If you have heard of a church with wall paintings and decide to make a special trip do not expect too much. Remember these paintings are very old and it has usually been

possible only to uncover and restore fragments of them.

If you find a set of paintings in near-perfect condition you should also be wary. The Victorians were very fond of repainting them when they found sufficiently strong outlines and the inexperienced church detective can easily confuse these reworkings with the medieval originals.

Some wall paintings are thought to date from as early as the twelfth century when wall paintings were often planned as complete schemes to cover all the inside walls of a church. In the following century rows of paintings were positioned one above the other on the church walls, while in the fourteenth century paintings were more often dedicated to devotional topics such as the Virgin Mary with the Christ child, or Jesus on the Cross. This was the period during which church wall paintings were at their most beautiful.

BELLS

Bells are fascinating things, if only because most of us hear them regularly but rarely see a peal in action.

The keen church detective will certainly want to get to know his local tower captain and see the bells being rung by climbing up to the belfry. This is really the only way to learn how they work but bells are very heavy and can be extremely dangerous if not handled properly so you should only investigate when a skilled bellringer is with you.

Nobody really knows how long bells have been used to call people to worship. Until the 1300s there was usually only one bell in a church, which was tolled to summon the villagers to worship and at the time of the Mass (the Sanctus bell). At this time bells were usually hung on a simple spindle and rung by pulling a rope attached to the spindle.

In the fourteenth century, ringers began to experiment with new ways of hanging the bell so that it could be more easily controlled. Bells began to be mounted on half wheels, with the rope attached to the rim of the wheel. Most parish churches at this time acquired two or three bells, while the larger churches often had eight or ten.

In medieval times the sound of bells was much more common than it is today. Bells were rung at baptisms, funerals, church festivals and even at military victories! They tolled for emergencies and it was believed that the clanging of bells could drive away the evil spirits of storm and tempest.

Before the Reformation a *Passing Bell* was tolled when a person was thought to be on the point of dying so that the clamour of the bell might clear the air of the demons who sought to clutch at a departing soul at its most vulnerable moment.

DO NOT TOUCH THE BELLS

In the seventeenth century bells were hung and tuned to a musical scale rather than just jangled at random. This led to the art of *change ringing* - introduced in 1668 by a Cambridge man called Fabian Stedman. Change ringing is virtually unknown outside this country. If you visit France, Italy or Germany with your parents or school you will generally only hear bells chimed. This means that they are not rung full circle like English peals and therefore they are unable to produce anything like the glorious sound of English church bells.

Chapter Eight

Fonts, Roods, Cells . . . and Mice

One of the joys of exploring old churches is that no two are ever the same. There are many features that are common to all but there are tremendous variations from church to church.

Why are some altars made of stone while others (in fact most) are wooden?

Why do pulpits vary so much?

And what are those funny flights of steps that appear to start in the middle of a wall but go nowhere?

ALTARS

If an altar is wooden it almost certainly dates from after about 1550. If it is made of stone (stone altars are sometimes known by the Latin name, *mensa*, meaning table) it could date from as early as the year 750. Early stone altars can be huge - as much as ten feet long and up to twelve inches thick. The huge mensa in the lovely Church of St Peter and St Paul at Northleach, Gloucestershire weighs a ton!

Sometimes altars are draped with colourful cloths called frontals. These frontals vary according to the Church year. For ordinary days the colour is green; for the chief feasts such as Christmas and Easter it is white; for periods of fasting such as Lent it is purple; and for days on which we remember Christian martyrs it is red.

Whatever the colour of the frontal it is likely to be covering what the church detective is keen to find out - whether the altar is made of wood or stone. You may therefore have to ask about the material the altar is made of.

If it is stone the priest or churchwarden might be willing to show you the consecration crosses which were usually carved into the mensa slab to denote the five wounds of Christ on the Cross - his two hands, two feet, and his side.

Keen church detectives might spot a mensa re-used (having been replaced as an altar by a wooden table) perhaps as a paving stone inside or outside the church, or even as a tombstone.

PULPITS

You might not think that there has been much change over the centuries in the style and appearance of pulpits, but you'd be wrong.

Around one hundred and sixty medieval pulpits survive in English churches, mainly in East Anglia and the West Country. The majority are wooden and date from the fifteenth century.

Whether made of wood or stone, pulpits are generally octagonal in shape. The panels of wooden ones were generally painted with saints or other figures. Early stone pulpits are usually supported on slender, tapering stems and give the impression with their delicate stonework of being rather tall and slender. They are often known as wine glass pulpits and are sometimes elaborately decorated.

In the eighteenth century one of the most amazing creations to be seen in English parish churches - the three-decker pulpit - came onto the scene. This was the age of the very long sermon, when it was the custom to equip the pulpit with an hour glass so that congregations could be sure they were getting their full measure! The three-decker pulpit had a box for the parish clerk on the ground floor, another above it for the minister when conducting the service, and on the highest level the pulpit, from where the Word of God was delivered at enormous length.

Even that was not the end, for above the preacher's head was a *sounding board* designed to be an aid to hearing. Another word for a sounding board is a tester. Sometimes in the eighteenth century they were crowned with an elaborate raised carving (such as the trumpeting angels in the churches at Molland and North Molton in Devon).

FONTS

Fonts are usually positioned near the entrance to a church. They are the receptacles for the water with which Christians are baptised signifying membership of God's Church.

There is a wonderful variety of fonts to be found in our churches and their styles represent all the great periods of church architecture.

Most fonts are made of stone, though for a time in the seventeenth and eighteen centuries it was the fashion to make tiny fonts in stone or metal set on tall wooden stands, rather like plant stands. If you spot a font made of lead, try drawing it: they are very rare.

Fonts dating from the thirteenth and fourteenth centuries are often decorated with carved foliage whereas the most impressive fifteenth century fonts are carved with angels, saints or figures representing the seven sacraments of the Church.

Font covers are usually wooden but you will not find a cover with every font. If you look carefully at any coverless medieval font you will probably see the marks in the stone where the cover has been forced off at a later date.

three-decker pulpit

ROODS

And now to those flights of disappearing steps. They were, in fact, the steps up to the rood loft.

Rood is the old English word for "cross". In many churches a massive beam was fixed above the entry into the chancel and this supported the rood, generally a very large cross. Often a figure of Christ was fixed to this flanked on either side by the Virgin Mary and John the Evangelist. In many churches which had a chancel screen, a rood loft was erected on top of it and a form of gallery built which effectively filled the space above the screen. Usually about six feet deep, these lofts were magnificently carved. They were used by the clergy and their assistants for special ceremonial occasions, especially on Palm Sunday. Access to the rood loft was usually by means of a turret stairway in the chancel arch or in the wall. Sometimes exterior stairs were built.

During the reign of the Protestant King Edward VI (1547-53) all roods were ordered to be destroyed. Today very few rood lofts remain occupying their original position, though some can be seen moved to the west end of the church where they were used as musicians' galleries, housing the church orchestra. Some of the finest remaining medieval rood lofts are in the churches at Atherington and Swimbridge in Devon, St Margaret's in Herefordshire, and Hubberholme in North Yorkshire. There are also quite a lot of fine examples in Wales.

MUSICIANS' GALLERIES

If you can't climb up to a rood loft you can at least take a closer look at the gallery in many old churches.

These are often fun to clamber round and quite often hold some interesting clues for the church detective. Look out for signs indicating that the gallery once housed a band or orchestra. From the seventeenth to the nineteenth centuries these were much more common than an organ in large numbers of country churches.

As a reminder of those days various musical instruments are still to be found in some churches. One of the oddest, still occasionally to be seen in a forgotten corner, is the vamp horn - a type of giant megaphone into which the "musician" hummed!

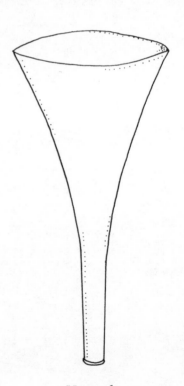

Vamp horn

It is often difficult to tell whether a particular gallery was used by a church orchestra or not. But at Parracombe old church in Devon there is no doubt. The remaining evidence ought to be clear to any church detective. Cut into the panelling in the cramped little west gallery is a large hole - just big enough to allow the base fiddle player the full sweep of his bow!

Old musical instruments are by no means the most eccentric items to be found in many parish churches. At Whitby, on the north-east coast of Yorkshire, the pulpit in the old parish church of St Mary has a sixteen foot high ear trumpet fixed to its side. It was positioned there in the early nineteenth century so that the vicar's wife, who was very deaf, could sit below and hear all of her husband's words of wisdom.

ANCHORITES' CELLS

Another oddity that the church detective should always be on the look out for is the possible site of a hermit's or anchorite's cell.

In the Middle Ages there were some rather eccentric people, both men and women, who chose to lead a holy, solitary existence in a small enclosed cell. The cells were usually built against the external wall of a church in lean-to form.

Known as "anchorites", these people were regarded with great awe by the ordinary people of the parish, who fed them through gaps in the walls of their cells, which they never left. Such was the devotion of these people to a solitary life of prayer and devotion that many regarded them as saints.

You will be extremely lucky - or clever - if you manage to find a church where it has been proved an anchorite's cell existed. However, if you visit the churches at Chipping Ongar and Lindsell in Essex you will find probably the best evidence of the

43

existence of these features that has been discovered so far.

Anchorites' cells are also thought to have existed in the churches of Tintagel in Cornwall, Chester-le-Street in Durham, Hartlip in Kent, St John the Baptist in Newcastle-upon-Tyne, Trunch in Norfolk, St Julian's in Norwich, Shere in Surrey, Hardham in Sussex and Skipton in Yorkshire. Experts believe there were hundreds of others, so there is plenty of scope for the church detective here!

AND MICE . . .

An altogether different oddity to be found in many parish churches in Yorkshire is the "family" of tiny wooden mice you will find carved into odd corners of the furniture. Look out for oak furniture dating from about 1920 onwards, and you will see plenty of these tiny wooden carved creatures.

They signify that the pew, or pulpit, or bench end, was the product of a famous Yorkshire craftsman, Robert Thompson, who established a renowned little firm that is still based in the village of Kilburn, twenty miles north of York.

Carved mice can be found in churches as far afield as Scotland and the South coast . . . but there is only one church in which you will find life-sized papier mache elephants' heads! You will find these at an old church in Berkshire, St Swithuns at Wickham near Hungerford. Here an eccentric Victorian squire brought the elephants' heads back from a trip to the Great Exhibition in Paris in 1855 and positioned them at the ends of eight large ceiling supports. They remain there to this day.

Chapter Nine

Lighter and Brighter – the New Plain Style

Apart from the early Norman and Saxon churches described in Chapter Two, all the churches and features described so far in this book have been in the *Gothic* style.

To be Gothic, ancient churches need to have been built between about 1200 and the early 1600s. But this was 400 years ago or more, so there are plenty of churches in this country that are old, but not built in a Gothic style.

We are going to finish by looking at these later churches because, as a church detective, you will want to know why the Gothic style came to an end and why many of the later churches are so different.

And different they certainly are - lighter, brighter and plainer. They have huge windows, with curved arches above, rather than the narrow windows with their pointed heads that characterise the earlier Gothic churches. They also have much plainer interiors and furnishings.

This was a totally new style. It came from a new way of thinking about art and architecture that actually had its roots in the buildings of ancient Greece and Rome. Today we call this movement, which began in Italy in about 1400, the "*Renaissance*". This is

a French word that means "new birth". And new birth - or "born again" to use a phrase that many Christians are fond of - is what these new Renaissance churches were all about.

All this new thinking took a while to filter across the Channel to this country, but in the 1500s many influential Englishmen were travelling on the continent and discovering these new styles of building and new ways of looking at life.

Many travellers were happy to be away from England at this time because under King Henry VIII, who reigned during 1509-47, there was enormous religious instability after the King rejected the Roman Catholic Church and founded the Church of England. This process - a very unhappy time for many in England because the Church was still central to most people's lives - was known as the Reformation. It was another reason why the style of church building began to change, because many people associated the Gothic style of building with the Roman Catholic Church that Henry had rejected, and wanted to move on to something different.

One of the foremost Englishmen who spent time in Europe was a designer and architect called Inigo Jones. He was born during the reign of Elizabeth I in about 1573 and died in 1652. He was an important man because he was Surveyor to the King's Works under King James I, who succeeded Elizabeth, and King Charles I.

In Italy Inigo Jones was captivated by the large, light, airy new buildings, and also fascinated by the fact that although they were newly built, they were based on the temples and other grand buildings of ancient Rome, in particular the rounded arch favoured by the Romans.

These Roman buildings were, in turn, based on the designs - mainly temples - of ancient Greece. So another key thing for you to know about these new lighter and brighter Renaissance churches is that they were *Classical* in design - because they had their origins in the ancient civilisations of Greece and Rome.

Inigo Jones returned to England very excited, and was responsible for the building of a very famous church - Classical in style - St Paul's in Covent Garden, London. Today this is known as the Actors' Church because it has many wall plaques commemorating famous actors. And memorial services to famous actors who die are still regularly held there.

This church was completed in 1633 and incorporated many of the ideas Inigo Jones brought back with him from Italy, especially its vast interior, with light pouring in from huge windows with plain glass and semi-circular heads on each side.

However, before Jones could build many more churches the Civil War broke out. During this period (1642-48) the whole country was in turmoil, and very few churches were built.

Inigo Jones died three years after the end of the war, but by this time there was a small group of very talented men in the principal universities who were the leaders in this country of this new way of looking at the world.

Foremost among these "new men" was Sir Christopher Wren (1632-1723), a professor at Oxford University.

Although his subject was astronomy, Wren was also a brilliant mathematician, and was fascinated by architecture. Early in his career, at the age of 32, he was responsible for the Sheldonian Theatre, one of the principal buildings at Oxford University.

However, he did not become well known as an architect until 1666, when he was called in by King Charles II after the great fire of London had destroyed huge numbers of buildings, among them many fine medieval churches.

Wren's task was to rebuild not only St Paul's Cathedral, but also 51 other churches in the City of London that had been destroyed by the fire. It was a huge task, in which he was assisted by other famous men of the time such as James Gibbs and Nicholas Hawksmoor.

Rather than rebuild slavish imitations in the old Gothic style Wren and his colleagues developed a new form of their own, heavily indebted to the discoveries of Inigo Jones and the temples of ancient Rome that he had so admired. Like the three phases of the Gothic style - Early English, Decorated and Perpendicular (see Chapter Two), the architecture of this period had its own distinctive elements, or orders. These were Doric, Ionic and Corinthian. These names date back to ancient Greece and can be recognised by the shapes of the pillars and the style of crowning features at the top - known as the capitals. Doric columns have capitals that are plain, round and simple. The Ionic order has capitals with curvy corners known as volutes. They make the corners of the capitals look rather like the horns of a ram. The Corinthian again has volutes, but the capitals also have spiky leaves (they are actually the acanthus plant) sprouting out and curling over at the points.

You will see all these styles in the churches of the City of London that were rebuilt by Wren and his contemporaries.

You can imagine the difficulty of turning what had originally been designs for classical temples into English parish churches. For a start they had to be adapted to suit our English climate. The buildings on which these new churches were based had no walls - just pillars - round the outside, as they were designed for a much hotter climate. The only walls were deep in the interior where the Roman priests gathered. Wren and his colleagues therefore had to adapt this style of building into Christian churches, enclosed with walls and seating a whole congregation.

The English architects proved well up to the task. Today there are 23 Wren churches still standing in the City, but all over the country you will find churches built in this new Classical style.

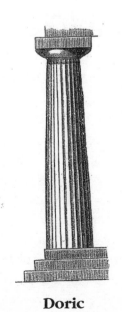

Doric

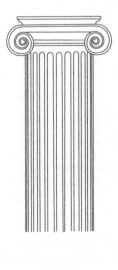

Ionic

Corinthian

as you will have read in Chapter Two, curved arches were favoured by the Normans in the eleventh and twelfth centuries. However, Norman arches in parish churches are generally small and narrow - totally different from the enormous plain-glazed round-headed and circular windows and huge double doorways favoured by Wren and his colleagues.

This Classical style persisted right through the following century - the 1700s. Then what do you think happened in the following century - the nineteenth century?

You've guessed it!

Soon after Queen Victoria came to the throne in 1837 pointed arches began to reappear in churches.

Why?

Well, just as the great "light and bright" churches of the Renaissance were felt by Christians at the time to indicate their understanding of God's world, so in Victorian times many leading thinkers believed that a fresh approach was needed.

These Victorian intellectuals believed that the Church of England had become sloppy and badly organised, and that the way to reform lay in rediscovering the true and powerful faith held by Christians in the Gothic Age. They firmly believed the great age of the Christian faith was in the late Middle Ages - the period, which began after the Norman phase, when the Gothic came in. The best way to express these views in their churches, they believed, lay in a return to the

You might think that reverting to the architectural styles of ancient Greece and Rome was going backwards and not being progressive at all. And,

architectural styles of this earlier, pre-Renaissance period.

So the Gothic returned. And all over the country it was back to the pointed arches and the spires of the Gothic Age - the only "true" architectural style in the opinion of those that held this view.

Today tastes have changed again. Very few churches are built in the Gothic style and the preference is generally for a plainer style of church building. This is probably just as well, because the plainer the style the cheaper the church is to build. The Gothic style, on the other hand, is expensive to build, and lower levels of church attendance have meant that church congregations, particularly those belonging to the Church of England, are poorer than they used to be. In addition modern building techniques mean that arches in church windows, doors and internal features today can be of almost any shape.

All these are reasons why, in the twenty-first century, we are seeing churches emerging as multi-purpose buildings, used for all sorts of purposes apart from worship. They are also often used by differing groups of Christians, who all hold services there at different times.

These are modern churches, and this book deals mainly with old churches, so we have come to the end of our voyage of discovery.

However, the keen church detective will have learned that in medieval times churches had many uses other than worship. Apart from the meetings and gatherings they are used for nowadays, churches in those far-off times were also used as places of defence when the town or village was under attack or siege by enemies, and for many other very ordinary purposes.

So with the arrival of the twenty-first-century multi-purpose churches you could, in a sense, say that, apart from all the materials they are built from, not a lot has changed!

Although this book aims to guide young people round old churches, it is interesting for church detectives to speculate on what the churches of the future will look like. One thing is sure - as long as Christians continue to believe in God and in his son Jesus Christ they will continue to build churches in which to worship Him.

Glossary

Altar: flat-topped table of stone or wood for the celebration of Holy Communion or the Eucharist and on which the main cross in the church and other objects of religious significance may be placed. Usually situated at the east end of the chancel.

Anchorite: religious hermit or solitary person who would live in an anchorite's cell, a small room attached to the church, which was sealed except for a hole through which food was passed, and a hole, called a *squint*, through which the anchorite could witness the celebration of Mass.

Arcade: series of arches supported by columns.

Buttress: masonry built against a wall to give extra strength.

Chancel: area at the east end of a church in which the altar is placed.

Clerestory: upper story of the nave wall rising above the roof of the aisles and pierced by windows to light the nave.

Corbel: supporting block of stone bonded into a wall, either inside or outside.

Corbel table: series of corbels, occurring just below the roof eaves externally or internally.

Crucifix: cross with figure of Christ attached to it.

Crypt: underground chamber, usually beneath the chancel.

Decorated: fourth of the English Gothic styles of church architecture, as defined by the architect Thomas Rickman (1776-1841). The Decorated period lasted from about 1280 to 1350.

Early English: period of English Gothic church architecture defined as from roughly 1200 to 1300.

Eaves: overhanging edge of a roof.

Fan vaulting: the most spectacular form of roof vaulting, usually associated with the late *Perpendicular* period.

Flying buttress: *buttress* in the form of an open half-arch which appears to lean against the wall of a church from the outside.

Font: container for the consecrated water used in baptism.

Galilee: small porch or chapel built against the west entrance of a church.

Gargoyle: projecting spout to carry water from the roof, generally carved as a grotesque face or animal.

Grotesque: stone carving in or on a church building in which the characters are deliberately carved in a ridiculous or deformed style.

Hammer beam: horizontal bracket projecting from a wall to give extra support to the roof timbers.

Lierne vault: complicated roof vaulting characteristic of the late Decorated period - when in a star formation called a stellar vault.

Lancet: tall narrow window, pointed at the top, characteristic of the *Early English* period.

Lychgate: roofed gateway into the churchyard where a coffin may be rested.

Medieval: term used to describe the period stretching from Saxon times to the mid-fifteenth century.

Mensa: stone altar.

Misericord: wooden bracket under the hinged seat in a choir stall - often bearing lively and imaginative carvings.

Mullions: vertical stone bars which divide a window into 'lights' or separate groups of glazed panels.

Perpendicular: period of English Gothic architecture from around 1350 to around 1550.

Rood: cross or crucifix supported on a loft or beam at the entrance to the chancel. The *rood screen* beneath may have a *rood loft* reached by a *rood stair*.

Sanctuary: area immediately around the main altar.

Squint: hole pierced in a wall to allow site of the altar. Also known as a hagioscope.

Vault: ceiling built of stone.

Tie-beam: main horizontal timber in a wooden roof that stretches across the church from one side wall to the other.

Tracery: intersecting stone or wooden ribwork in the upper part of a window or screen.

Transom: horizontal bar of stone across a window.

Weepers: small figures set in niches around the sides of a tomb.

THE NATIONAL SOCIETY

A Christian Voice in Education

The National Society (Church of England) for Promoting Religious Education is a charity which supports all those involved in Christian education - teachers and school governors, students and parents, clergy and lay people - with the resources of its RE Centres, archives, courses and conferences.

Founded in 1811, the Society was chiefly responsible for setting up the nationwide network of Church schools in England and Wales and still provides grants for building projects and legal and administrative advice for headteachers and governors. It now publishes a wide range of books, pamphlets and audio-visual items, and two magazines **Crosscurrent** and **Together**.

For details of membership of the Society please contact the Promotions Secretary, The National Society, Church House, Great Smith Street, London SW1P 3NZ.

THE CHURCH DETECTIVE'S NOTEBOOK

Use these pages to record any extra information you discover as you
go church crawling . . .